DISCOVERING ANCIENT GREECE

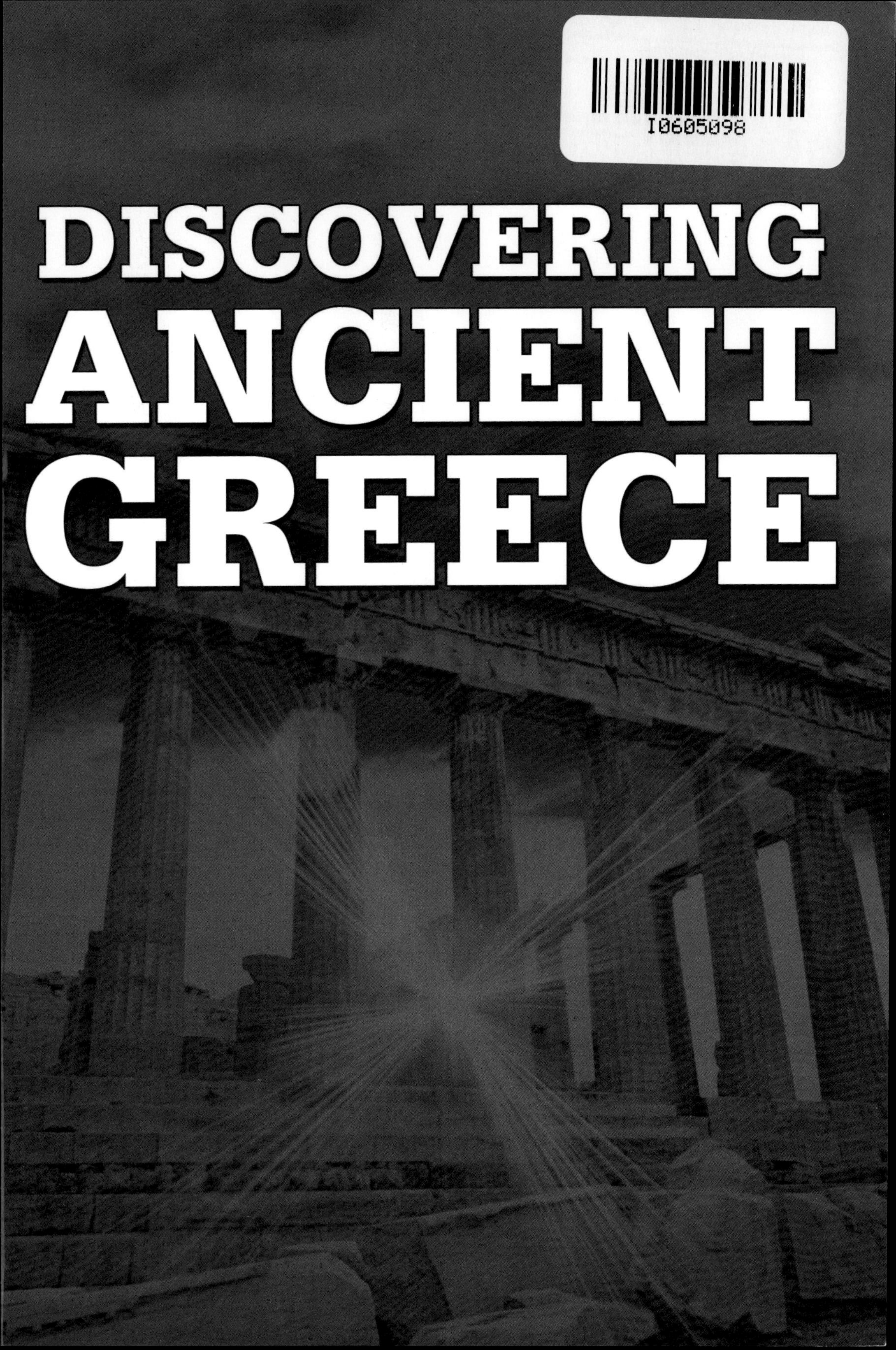

EXPLORING ANCIENT CIVILIZATIONS

DISCOVERING ANCIENT GREECE

KATHRYN MORGAN

Britannica Educational Publishing
IN ASSOCIATION WITH
ROSEN
EDUCATIONAL SERVICES

Published in 2015 by Britannica Educational Publishing (a trademark of Encyclopædia Britannica, Inc.)
in association with The Rosen Publishing Group, Inc.
29 East 21st Street, New York, NY 10010

Distributed exclusively by Rosen Publishing.
To see additional Britannica Educational Publishing titles, go to rosenpublishing.com.

First Edition

Britannica Educational Publishing
J. E. Luebering: Director, Core Reference Group
Anthony L. Green: Editor, Compton's by Britannica

Rosen Publishing
Hope Lourie Killcoyne: Executive Editor
Jacob R. Steinberg: Editor
Nelson Sá: Art Director
Michael Moy: Designer
Cindy Reiman: Photography Manager

Library of Congress Cataloging-in-Publication Data

Morgan, Kathryn, 1983–
Discovering ancient Greece/Kathryn Morgan.
pages cm.—(Exploring ancient civilizations)
Includes bibliographical references and index.
ISBN 978-1-62275-836-4 (library bound) — ISBN 978-1-62275-835-7 (pbk.) —
ISBN 978-1-62275-834-0 (6-pack)
1. Greece—Civilization—To 146 B.C.—Juvenile literature. I. Title.
DF77.M7585 2015
938—dc23

2014024100

Manufactured in the United States of America

Cover, pp. 1, 3 Christian Delbert/Shutterstock.com; p. 7 © North Wind Picture Archives/The Image Works; p. 9 Dorling Kindersley/Getty Images; pp. 10, 13 De Agostini/Getty Images; p. 11 © akg-images/Peter Connolly/The Image Works; p. 16 V-DIA-Scala from Art Resource, NY; pp. 17, 40 Alinari/Art Resource, NY; p.19 Mondadori Portfolio/Hulton Fine Art Collection/Getty Images; p. 21 © v0v/Fotolia; p. 24 Danita Delimont/Gallo Images/Getty Images; p. 26 Album/Prisma/SuperStock; p. 27 Hemis.fr/SuperStock; p. 29 Erich Lessing/Art Resource, NY; p. 30 Galleria degli Uffizi, Florence, Italy/Bridgeman Images; p. 32 Photos.com/Thinkstock; p. 33 Panagiotis Karapanagiotis/iStock/Thinkstock; pp. 35, 42 DEA/G. Dagli Orti/De Agostini Picture Library/Getty Images; p. 36 The Bridgeman Art Library/Getty Images; pp. 38–39 Scala/Art Resource, NY; cover and interior graphics Freckles/Shutterstock.com (patterned banners and borders, background textures), HorenkO/Shutterstock.com (background textures).

CONTENTS

INTRODUCTION

More than three thousand years ago, the Greeks began to develop one of the most remarkable civilizations of the ancient world. In their own time, the ancient Greeks spread their influence far and wide by expanding their borders beyond the Greece we know today. They founded cities along the coasts of Africa, Turkey, Italy, and France, carrying their culture throughout the region. But their impact did not end there. Their achievements in politics, philosophy, science, and the arts formed a legacy that has had an unmatched influence on Western civilization to this day.

The ancient Greeks lived in self-governing communities called city-states. In the most famous of the city-states, Athens, they created the world's first democracy. The word "democracy" comes from a Greek word meaning "rule by the people." Democracy is still one of the most widely used political systems in the world.

Though often separated by barriers of sea and mountain, the city-states were united by their common language, religion, and customs. They also shared a body of stories about their gods, heroes, and the nature of the universe. These stories, or myths, have

As shown on this map, the boundaries of ancient Greece—and the extent of its influence—went beyond the borders of the modern country of Greece.

influenced world literature and continue to be studied today. With such an interesting culture ready to be explored, let the discovery of ancient Greece begin!

CHAPTER ONE
DAILY LIFE

Like most cultures of the ancient world, Greece had a class system that grouped people into distinct social rankings. The hierarchy of privilege and authority placed naturally born Greeks, particularly men, at the top. Beneath them were residents who had relocated from other countries, called metics. They shared many of the obligations of native Greeks, but they were denied certain benefits of citizenship. The class of metics also included freed slaves. Slaves formed the lowest class. They possessed no rights and, like metics and freedmen, were not considered citizens.

The Only True Citizens: Greek Men

Because adult male citizens formed the upper class, they dominated public life in ancient Greece. In the city-states with a democratic form of government, only adult males could take part in politics. These men represented just a small portion of the population. In Athens—the best-known city-state and the birthplace of democracy—they made up only 12 percent of the people.

Athenian men spent their time talking politics and philosophy in the agora, or marketplace. They exercised in the athletic fields, performed military duty, and took part in state festivals. Some took part in the Assembly, which made the city-state's laws and policies. Despite their high social standing, even men were not allowed to publicly criticize their government or the gods.

In the military, men were trained to think and act tactically. Athens developed a powerful navy

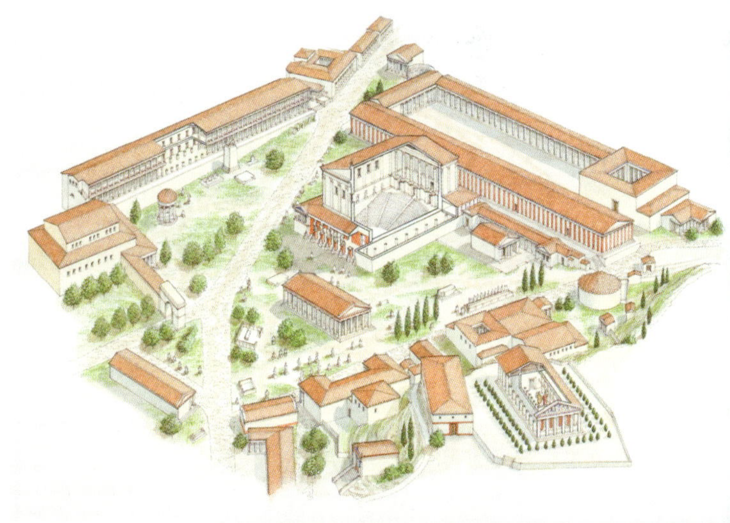

This illustration shows the layout of the agora of Athens. In ancient Greek cities, the agora was an open space that served as a meeting ground for various activities of the citizens.

A ceramic plate depicts a battle between Menelaus, king of Sparta, and the Trojan hero Hector. In the legendary conflict known as the Trojan War, the early Greeks defeated the people of Troy.

and became a strong sea power. But the most powerful military city-state was Sparta, with its superior army. All male Spartan citizens between the ages of twenty and sixty served in the army.

Life at Home: Women and Children

Women in ancient Greece spent their days at home. They spun, wove, and performed other household chores. The houses were made of sun-dried brick and stood on narrow, winding streets. There were usually several rooms surrounding a private courtyard. The rooms included separate apartments for men and women as well as tiny bedrooms.

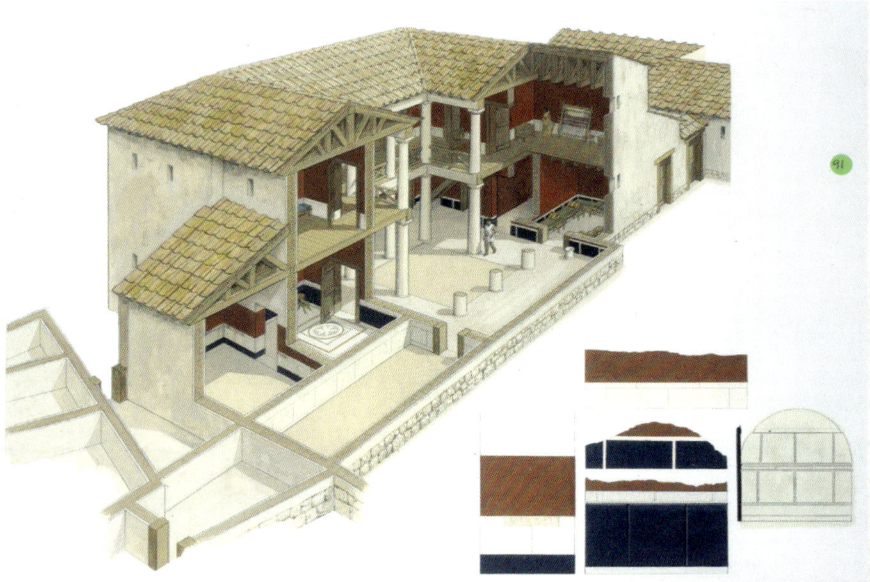

Homes in ancient Greece were designed around a courtyard that provided a place for women to enjoy fresh air and for children to play. They also included separate living quarters for men and women.

The courtyard allowed women to enjoy the outdoors without leaving the home and also provided a place for the children to play. Children in ancient Greece had many of the same kinds of toys that children today play with. These included rattles, clay animals, horses pulled on a string, yo-yos, and dolls.

EDUCATION IN ANCIENT GREECE

School in ancient Greece was different from what we are used to today. Boys typically went to school at age seven. In Athens, boys studied math and science, as well as reading and writing, music, literature, and debate. Girls in Athens did not attend school. Instead, their mothers taught them how to sew, cook, and run a household.

In Sparta, boys were taught to be soldiers. Instead of learning music and literature, they were drilled each day in gymnastics and military exercises. They learned to endure pain and hardship without complaint and to obey orders absolutely and without question. Even the girls in Sparta learned to be warriors. They were trained to wrestle, fistfight, and handle a weapon in case they needed to protect Sparta while the men were away at war.

Servitude: Life as a Slave

Slave labor produced much of the wealth that gave the citizens of Athens time and money to pursue art and learning and to serve the state. Slaves in ancient Greece were not born into servitude. Most were foreigners captured in war or kidnapped in "barbarian," or non-Greek, lands.

A slave guiding a chariot is depicted on this fresco from the vaulted ceiling of an ancient Greek tomb in what is now Bulgaria.

A slave was not permitted to get married or to have children without the approval of his or her owner. Female slaves often acted as nannies to the children. They also carried out general housework such as cooking and cleaning. Male slaves were required to do outdoor jobs such as working in the fields, caring for horses, acting as handymen, or gardening. Slaves also accompanied their owners' children to and from school.

In Athens, slaves often had a chance to obtain their freedom, for quite frequently they were paid for their work, and this gave them a chance to save money. After a slave had bought his or her freedom or had been set free by a grateful master, he or she joined the class of metics, or resident aliens. Many of the slaves, however, had miserable lives. They were sent in gangs into the silver mines, working in narrow underground corridors by the dim light of little lamps.

CHAPTER TWO

MYTHS

The ancient Greeks used stories to explain the world around them. Some of these stories involved powerful gods while others told of great heroes. Today these stories are called myths. Like the myths of many other cultures, those of ancient Greece tell how the world was created and help explain why things happen. The ancient Greeks also treated their myths as guides for what was right and wrong. They believed that if the lessons weren't followed, the gods would become angry and the people would be punished.

Gods and Goddesses

In ancient Greek myths, twelve major gods and goddesses ruled from Mount Olympus. Each one embodied or controlled specific natural forces or

Mount Olympus is the highest mountain peak in Greece and, in Greek mythology, was the home of the gods.

areas of life. The chief god was Zeus, a sky god who made thunder and lightning, rain, and the winds. Hades and Poseidon were Zeus's brothers. Poseidon ruled over the sea, while Hades ruled over the underworld. The Olympian gods also included several sons of Zeus. Ares was the god of war. Apollo presided over religious and civil law and was the god of light, music, poetry, healing, and prophecy. Hermes was the messenger of the gods as well as the god of roads, travelers, dreams, and thieves. Hephaestus was the god of fire and metalworking.

Among the Olympian goddesses was Hera, the sister and wife of Zeus. She was the goddess of marriage and of women. Zeus's sister Hestia was the goddess of the home and family. Athena, Zeus's favorite daughter, was the goddess of wisdom. Artemis, Apollo's twin sister, was the Moon goddess as well as the goddess of the hunt and of wild animals. Aphrodite was the goddess of love.

In addition to these twelve major gods, there were numerous lesser ones. Demeter, for instance, was the goddess of grain. Dionysus was the god of wine and fruitfulness. Pan was a rural god of fertility. Asclepius was the god of medicine.

A painting on an ancient Greek cup depicts the gods on Mount Olympus. The gods visible here are, from left to right, Athena, Zeus, Dionysus, Hera, and Aphrodite.

TITANS

The Titans, also known as the elder gods, ruled the world before Zeus and the rest of the Olympian gods. They were the children of Earth (Gaea) and the heavens (Uranus). Uranus hated the Titans, and he imprisoned them inside Gaea's body (that is, inside Earth). Led by Cronus, the Titans rebelled against Uranus. After they took power, Cronus ruled as the chief god. Eventually, however, Zeus, one of Cronus's sons, in turn rebelled against him. For ten years, the Titans fought against the Olympian gods, but they lost. Zeus then became the chief god. According to many myths, the Titans were banished to Tartarus, the deepest region of the underworld.

Heroes and Monsters

The ancient Greeks also told stories about heroes, human beings who performed amazing feats. Hero myths included elements from tradition, folktales, and fiction. Many heroes endured long journeys, battled in wars, or fought against monsters. The hero Perseus killed Medusa, one of the Gorgons, who were winged female monsters with snakes for hair. Anyone who looked at Medusa turned into

This mosaic floor depicts the monster Medusa, who had snakes for hair. Any person who looked at Medusa was turned into stone.

stone. Using his shield as a mirror, Perseus cut off her head. Out of her blood was born the famous winged horse, Pegasus.

Another famous story is that of the Minotaur, a monster with the body of a man and the head of a bull. It was the offspring of Pasiphae, the wife of King Minos of Crete, and a bull sent to Minos by the god Poseidon for sacrifice. Minos, instead of sacrificing it, kept it alive. As a punishment, Poseidon made Pasiphae fall in love with it and bear its child. To protect his people, Minos had the Minotaur locked up in a labyrinth, or maze. The king then ordered that seven boys and seven girls from Athens would periodically be sacrificed to the Minotaur, who ate only human flesh. One day the Athenian hero Theseus volunteered to be sacrificed. With the help of Ariadne, daughter of Minos and Pasiphae, he killed the monster, thereby freeing Athens from its tribute.

Most of the heroes in ancient Greece were given weapons or advice by the gods. Some were even the children of gods. One such hero was Heracles. He was a son of Zeus and gifted with great strength. Tricked into killing his own family, Heracles had to perform twelve labors, or tasks, to earn forgiveness from the gods. One famous task was to slay the Hydra, a serpent with nine heads. Each time Heracles cut off one head, two more would grow back in its place. To prevent the heads from growing back, Heracles's nephew held a torch to the Hydra's neck to burn out the roots. This allowed Heracles to slay it once and for all.

This statue shows Heracles battling the nine-headed Hydra as one of the twelve labors he performed to placate the gods.

Lasting Influence

The myths of ancient Greece have remained unrivaled in the Western world as sources of imaginative ideas for art and literature. Painters, sculptors, poets, and other writers from ancient times to the present have been inspired by Greek mythology. They discovered that the stories' themes

ROMAN GODS AND GODDESSES

The ancient Romans adopted much of their mythology from ancient Greece. Many of the gods and goddesses of ancient Greece have a counterpart with a different name in Roman myths.

Greek Name	Roman Name
Zeus	Jupiter
Hera	Juno
Poseidon	Neptune
Athena	Minerva
Artemis	Diana
Ares	Mars
Aphrodite	Venus
Hermes	Mercury

Even some Greek heroes had a corresponding Roman name. Heracles was known as Hercules in Rome.

were still significant and relevant for the people of their time. Artists and writers have borrowed elements from the myths, retelling ancient stories in modern ways.

CHAPTER THREE

GOVERNMENT

In ancient times, Greece was not a country in the modern sense but a collection of several hundred independent cities, each with its surrounding countryside. Since these cities were independent political units, they are known as city-states. In Greek, the word for "city-state" is *polis*, and the English word "politics" comes from it. Each city-state was a self-governing community capable of maintaining its independence by enlisting its men as soldiers.

The independence of the city-states led to great diversity in the size, prosperity, culture, and forms of government among them. Some were democracies; others were governed by kings, tyrants, or small groups. What the city-states had in common was their independence and the fact that they were governed by laws.

Types of Government

The government of many city-states passed through four stages. During the eighth and seventh centuries BCE, the kings disappeared. Monarchy gave way to oligarchy—that is, rule by a few. The oligarchic successors of the kings were the wealthy landowning nobles, the eupatridae, or wellborn. However, the rivalry among these nobles and the discontent of the oppressed masses was so great that soon a third stage appeared.

Periander (died *c.* 587 BCE) was the second tyrant of the Greek city-state of Corinth. A firm and effective ruler, he exploited his city's commercial and cultural potential. Unlike today, the Greeks did not use "tyrant" in a negative sense.

The third type of government was known as tyranny. A eupatrid would seize absolute power, usually by promising the people to right the wrongs inflicted upon them by the other landholding eupatridae. He was known as a tyrant. Among the Greeks this was not a negative term; it merely meant one who had seized kingly power without the qualification of royal descent. The tyrants of the seventh century were a stepping-stone to democracy, or rule by the people. It was the tyrants who taught the people their rights and power.

TYPES OF DEMOCRACY

The type of democracy used in Athens is called a direct democracy. In a direct democracy, all citizens are given the chance to discuss and vote on laws. This form of democracy was possible in Athens because of the city-state's relatively small size, which allowed all of the citizens (adult male Greeks) to gather together in the Assembly.

This form of democracy is different from the type practiced today in most places, where the populations are much larger. In a representative democracy, the citizens choose a smaller group of people to represent them in the legislature and pass laws on their behalf.

Athens

By the beginning of the fifth century BCE, Athens had gone through these stages and emerged as the first democracy in the history of the world. There was no president or prime minister of Athens. In its period of democracy, the chief officials—known as archons—were chosen by lot. The heart of the Athenian government was the Assembly, which met almost weekly to decide the city-state's laws and policies. All adult male

In this twentieth-century engraving, William Spencer Bagdatopoulos depicted the Athenian Assembly, a loosely organized, often tumultuous democratic body of about five thousand male citizens who debated and voted on political matters.

citizens of Athens could participate in the Assembly, though typically only about five thousand of the thirty thousand or so eligible men attended. After discussion that was open to all members, the Assembly voted by a show of hands. A simple majority prevailed.

The agenda of the Assembly was set by a body known as the Council of Five Hundred. Unlike the Assembly, it was composed of representatives. The five hundred members of the Council were ordinary male citizens who were chosen by lot to represent their district for a one-year term. Each district was allotted a certain number of representatives in rough proportion to its population. The Council's use of representatives (though chosen by lot rather than by election) foreshadowed the election of representatives in later democratic systems.

Sparta

The government of Sparta was very different from that of Athens. Sparta had a type of government known as an oligarchy, which puts a small number of people in power. The Spartan government was headed by two kings who ruled jointly. Laws were made by the council of elders, which consisted of the two kings and twenty-eight other men over the age of sixty. Laws put forth by the council passed to an assembly made up of all Spartan citizens—free adult males. The assembly was generally expected to approve the council's proposals.

This statue of the Spartan king Leonidas I stands in the modern city of Sparta, Greece. Leonidas is known for leading a greatly outnumbered Greek force of seven thousand men against a Persian invasion during the Battle of Thermopylae—a battle the Greeks ultimately lost.

The Spartan government also included five ephors, or overseers. They balanced the power of the kings and the council of elders. They presided over meetings of the council of elders and the assembly and were responsible for the execution of the laws. The ephors were responsible for judging crimes and punishment and could even arrest and imprison a king. Unlike the kings and the council, the ephors were elected annually.

CHAPTER FOUR
PHILOSOPHY

Philosophy and debate were important in ancient Greece, especially in Athens. The word "philosophy" itself comes from a Greek word meaning "love of wisdom." The thinkers of ancient Greece had an immeasurable influence not only on philosophy but also on Western society as a whole. There were many Greek philosophers, but three names tower above the rest: Socrates, Plato, and Aristotle.

Socrates

Socrates ranks as one of the world's greatest moral teachers. Challenging the ideas of thinkers who came before, he believed it is possible to learn absolute virtue and attain truth. He dedicated himself to uncovering the nature of virtue and to finding a rule of life. Interested in

Raphael's *The School of Athens*, with Plato and Aristotle at the center, is a symbolic painting suggesting the philosophical dominance of Athens in the ancient world.

neither money, nor fame, nor power, Socrates wandered the streets of Athens talking to whoever would listen. He asked questions, criticized answers, and poked holes in faulty arguments. Though he wrote nothing himself, his ideas were preserved by his admirers—most notably the philosopher Plato.

Socrates, however, was not appreciated by the Athenian mob and its self-serving leaders.

Jacques-Louis David's oil painting *The Death of Socrates* (*c.* 1787) illustrates the scene of Socrates's death by poisoning.

His genius for exposing pompous frauds made him many enemies. At last, three of his political foes charged him with "neglect of the gods" and "corruption of the young." They were false charges, but politically convenient. Socrates was sentenced to death by poisoning by a jury of his fellow citizens.

THE SOCRATIC METHOD

The Socratic method is an educational strategy that involves a series of questions and answers between a teacher and a student. It is named after Socrates and based on his style of instruction. The Socratic method is used to challenge ideas that people take for granted or assume are true. Socrates used this type of dialogue to examine concepts such as virtue, courage, piety, and justice.

Such question-and-answer conversations are still used in classrooms today, particularly in law schools. The goal is either to help students reach a satisfactory answer or to realize the limitations of their knowledge. With this method, students learn critical thinking, reasoning, and logic by first finding weaknesses in their arguments and then strengthening them.

Plato

Plato was Socrates's foremost pupil and recorder of many of his conversations. He wrote more than thirty works called dialogues. These were presented mostly in conversational style as discussions between Socrates and his friends. Plato developed a many-sided philosophy that includes a

A bust of the Greek philosopher Plato is displayed in one of the Capitoline Museums in Rome. Plato is best known for his work the *Republic*.

theory of knowledge, a theory of human conduct, a theory of the state, and a theory of the universe. His most famous work is the *Republic*, which is one of the masterpieces of world literature. It discusses the nature of justice and describes Plato's ideal society.

Plato's Academy at Athens, which opened in about 387 BCE, was the first forerunner of today's colleges and universities. It was a school devoted to philosophy, law, and scientific research—primarily mathematics. It remained in operation for more than nine hundred years.

Aristotle

If Plato was the successor to Socrates, then the next in line after Plato was his own student Aristotle. Unlike Socrates and Plato, Aristotle did not grow up in Athens. He lived in Macedonia, in northern Greece, where his father was a friend and the physician of the king. As a teenager, Aristotle moved to Athens, where he enrolled at Plato's Academy. He threw himself wholeheartedly into Plato's pursuit of truth and goodness. Plato was soon calling him the "mind of the school." Aristotle stayed at the Academy for twenty years as a student and teacher. Then he returned to the Macedonian court to tutor a prince, who grew up to become the famed conqueror Alexander the Great.

Aristotle eventually started his own school in Athens, the Lyceum. He led his pupils in research in every existing field of knowledge. One of Aristotle's most important contributions was defining and classifying the various branches of knowledge. He sorted them into physics, metaphysics, psychology, rhetoric, poetics, and logic, and thus laid the foundation of most of the sciences of today.

A statue of Aristotle stands in his birthplace of Stagira, Greece. The successor to Plato in Greek philosophy, Aristotle defined and classified all existing branches of knowledge, including physics, logic, and poetics.

CHAPTER FIVE

THE ARTS

The ancient Greeks reached their creative peak in Athens in the fifth century BCE. This was the great era of Greek philosophy, literature, architecture, and sculpture. In all of their arts, the Greeks were guided above all else by reason. "Nothing to excess" was their central doctrine, a doctrine that the Roman poet Horace later interpreted as "the golden mean."

Literature

The ancient Greeks created a literature of such brilliance that it has rarely been equaled and never surpassed. In poetry, tragedy, comedy, and history, Greek writers created masterpieces that have inspired, influenced, and challenged readers to the present day.

At the beginning of Greek literature stand the two epic poems of Homer, the *Iliad* and the

Odyssey. The figure of Homer is shrouded in mystery. Although the works as they now stand are credited to him, it is certain that their roots reach far back before his time. The *Iliad* is the famous story about the Trojan War, a legendary conflict between the early Greeks and the people of Troy. The *Odyssey* tells the story of Odysseus, king of Ithaca, who wanders for ten years trying to get home after the Trojan War.

This is a marble bust of Homer by an unknown artist.

The ancient Greeks invented drama and produced enduring masterpieces in both tragedy and comedy. The three great tragic playwrights were Aeschylus, Sophocles, and Euripides. The plays of Aeschylus focus on the conflicting concerns of political leaders for their people and for themselves. Sophocles is

As narrated in *Oedipus the King*, Oedipus meets a monster called the Sphinx and must correctly answer its riddle or be devoured. Upon solving the Sphinx's riddle, Oedipus becomes king of Thebes and is married to Queen Jocasta, unaware that she is his mother. Part of the legend is portrayed here in Jean-Auguste-Dominique Ingres' painting *Oedipus and the Sphinx* (1808).

best known for *Oedipus the King* (also called *Oedipus Rex*); it tells the story of Oedipus, who unwittingly kills his father and marries his mother. The tragedies of Euripides focus on common people, rather than heroic legendary figures, and explore the sorrow and suffering in human life.

Among the best comic playwrights of ancient Greece were Aristophanes and Menander. The plays of Aristophanes are notable for their raucous humor and bold political criticism. Menander's comedies concentrate on characters from ordinary life, presenting such figures as stern fathers, young lovers, and conspiring slaves.

Two of the best historians to have ever written flourished in ancient Greece. Herodotus is commonly called the father of history, and his *History* contains the first truly literary use of prose in Western literature. Thucydides, however, was a better historian. His critical use of sources, inclusion of documents, and extensive research made his *History of the Peloponnesian War* a significant influence on later generations of historians.

Architecture

The finest examples of Greek architecture were temples. For centuries the Greeks erected permanent stone buildings almost exclusively for religious monuments. Their temples were statue chambers containing a god's sacred image.

There are two types of Greek temple: the Ionic, evolved in Ionia on the eastern shore of the Aegean Sea, and the Doric, evolved on the western shore. The two systems are called orders because their parts and proportions are ordered and coordinated. Both show the same basic plan: a central windowless statue chamber; a porch, usually with two columns in front; and a ring of columns, the peristyle, around the four sides.

The Ionic and Doric temples differ in their details. The Doric temple is simple in plan, the Ionic larger with a double peristyle. The columns are also distinct: the Doric has a dish-shaped top, or capital, and no base, while the Ionic has paired scrolls at its capital and carved rings at its base. Later the

The simple beauty of Doric columns can be seen on the Greek temple at Segesta, Sicily, dating from about 424–416 BCE.

Greeks added a third type of column, the Corinthian. It was a variation of the Ionic with realistic leaves of the acanthus plant on its capital.

THE ACROPOLIS

The most beautiful temples and statues of ancient Greece stood upon the Acropolis, a small plateau in the heart of Athens. The most prominent structure is the Parthenon, built between 447 and 438 BCE. This large, richly decorated temple was dedicated to Athena and contained a huge statue of the goddess. The Erechtheum, with its caryatids—or marble female figures—supporting the roof, and the Temple of Athena Nike were also built on the Acropolis during the same period. This collection of temples was approached through the Propylaea, a large entrance building. The Theater of Dionysus, at the southern base of the Acropolis, was the city's drama center.

Housed in the Louvre Museum in Paris, France, *Diana of Versailles* depicts the Greek goddess of the hunt, Artemis (called Diana by the Romans), in the marble typical of ancient Greek sculptures.

Sculpture and Painting

By the fifth century BCE Greek sculptors had solved many of the problems that faced earlier artists. They had learned to represent the human form naturally and easily, in action or at rest. They were interested chiefly in portraying gods, however.

The greatest name in Greek sculpture is that of Phidias. Under his direction the sculptures decorating the Parthenon were planned and executed. Some of them may have been the work of his own hand. His great masterpieces were the huge gold and ivory statue of Athena that stood within this temple and the similar one of Zeus in the temple at Olympia.

The Greeks had plenty of beautiful marble and used it freely for their sculpture. They were not satisfied with its cold whiteness, however, and thus painted their statues. Some statues have been found with their bright colors still preserved, but most of them lost their paint through weathering. The works of the great Greek painters have disappeared completely, and we know only what ancient writers tell us about them. Parrhasius, Zeuxis, and Apelles, the great painters of the fourth century BCE, were famous for their interesting use of color.

Much of what we know about Greek painting is derived from the paintings that decorated ancient Greek vases. In this example, Nike drives a four-horse chariot with Heracles by her side as Hermes stands before them.

Fortunately, many examples of Greek vases have survived. The beautiful decorations on these vases give us some idea of Greek painting. They are examples of the wonderful feeling for form and line that made the Greeks supreme in the field of sculpture.

Conclusion

Ancient Greek civilization—"the glory that was Greece," in the words of American writer Edgar Allan Poe—was short-lived and confined to a very small geographic area. Yet it has influenced Western civilization far out of proportion to its size and duration.

The Greece that Poe praised was primarily Athens during its golden age in the fifth century BCE. The English poet John Milton called Athens "the eye of Greece, mother of arts and eloquence." Athens attracted those who wanted to work, speak, and think in an environment of freedom. In its lofty atmosphere were born ideas about human nature and political society that are fundamental to the Western world today.

GLOSSARY

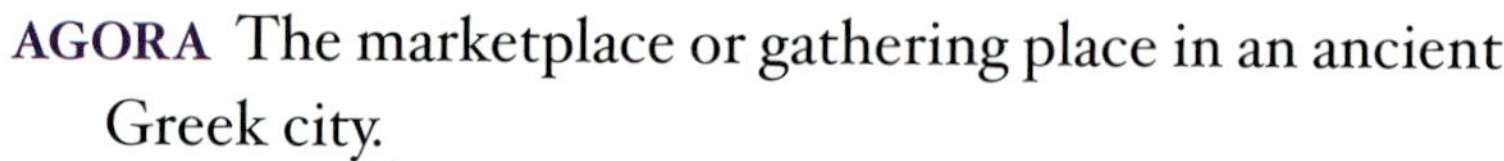

AGORA The marketplace or gathering place in an ancient Greek city.

CITY-STATE An independent state consisting of a city and the surrounding territory.

DIRECT DEMOCRACY A form of democracy practiced in small communities in which all (or nearly all) citizens gather together in an assembly to pass laws or adopt policies by a majority vote of all those present.

EPHOR One of the group of five highest Spartan officials who, with the kings, formed the main executive wing of the state.

HIERARCHY A system in which people or things are ranked one above another.

HYDRA A nine-headed serpent in Greek mythology that was killed by Heracles.

METIC Resident foreigner in an ancient Greek city-state who held some civil privileges.

OLIGARCHY A government controlled by a small group of people.

PIETY Devotion to a god or gods.

PLACATE To calm the anger or bitterness of.

REPRESENTATIVE DEMOCRACY A form of democracy in which citizens elect representatives to pass laws on the citizens' behalf.

SERVITUDE The condition of being a slave.

SURPASS To become better, greater, or stronger than.

TACTICALLY Showing skillful planning in order to accomplish a goal, as in war.

TRIBUTE A payment by one ruler or state to another in acknowledgment of submission or as the price of protection.

Bensinger, Henry. *Ancient Greek Daily Life*. New York, NY: Powerkids Press, 2014.

Bensinger, Henry. *Ancient Greek Government*. New York, NY: PowerKids Press, 2014.

Burns, Kylie. *Sparta!* New York, NY: Crabtree Publishing, 2013.

Connor, George. *Zeus: King of the Gods*. New York, NY: First Second, 2010.

Hawthorne, Nathaniel. *A Wonder-Book: Heroes and Monsters of Greek Mythology*. Mineola, NY: Dover Publications, 2013.

Landmann, Bimba. *The Fate of Achilles: Text Inspired by Homer's* Iliad *and Other Stories of Ancient Greece*. Los Angeles, CA: J. Paul Getty Museum, 2011.

Lente, Fred Van, and Alexey Aparin. *Hercules*. New York, NY: Osprey Publishing, 2013.

Marcovitz, Hal. *Ancient Greece*. San Diego, CA: ReferencePoint Press, 2013.

Samson, Donald, and Adam Agee. *At the Hot Gates: An Account of the Battle of Thermopylae*. Chatham, NY: Association of Waldorf Schools, 2012.

Stafford, Emma J. *Exploring the Life, Myth, and Art of Ancient Greece*. New York, NY: Rosen Central, 2012.

Villing, Alexandra. *The Ancient Greeks: Their Lives and Their World*. Los Angeles, CA: J. Paul Getty Museum, 2010.

Websites

Because of the changing nature of Internet links, Rosen Publishing has developed an online list of websites related to the subject of this book. This site is updated regularly. Please use this link to access this list:

http://www.rosenlinks.com/ANCIV/Gree

Index

R

S

T

U

V

W

Z